PERSUADE
WITH A STORY!

HOW TO
ATTRACT CLIENTS
AND CUSTOMERS
*With Heroic
Storytelling*

HENRY J. DEVRIES

INDIE BOOKS
INTERNATIONAL

ISBN: 1-941870-65-1
ISBN 13: 978-1-941870-65-5
Library of Congress Control Number: 2016910801

Designed by Joni McPherson, mcphersongraphics.com

INDIE BOOKS INTERNATIONAL, LLC
2424 VISTA WAY, SUITE 316
OCEANSIDE, CA 92054

www.indiebooksintl.com

*To my Indie Books International Family
and Friends*

Our brand is generosity, family, and growth.

*This book is also dedicated to the memory of
my mom and dad, Jack and Janice DeVries,
who encouraged me to finish and publish my
fiction stories one day (sorry you never lived to
see that), and to the matriarch of our family,
the beloved Aunt Carla Lee DeVries, who had
a wacky idea in 1936 in Berlin that created
an international incident. But that is another
story for another time.*

[PREFACE]

In 1857 Henry David Thoreau wrote a letter to a friend that offered commentary about story length:

> *"Not that the story need be long, but it will take a long while to make it short."*

Dear Reader: I took the time to write you a short book instead of a long one. Remember, like TNT, great power can come in a small package.

Henry J. DeVries
June, 2016

[CONTENTS]

Appendix

"We're adjusting our dress code to facilitate greater diversity.
Who's your favorite Star Wars character?"

[CHAPTER 1]
The Quest to
PERSUADE WITH
A STORY

Humans are hardwired for stories. Storytelling helps business leaders persuade on an emotional level. Maybe that is why companies like FedEx, Kimberly-Clark, and Microsoft are hiring storytelling experts to teach their executives to tell relatable stories.

Nothing is as persuasive as storytelling with a purpose. In this little book are the keys to proven techniques for telling a great story employed by Hollywood, Madison Avenue, and Wall Street.

In addition to humorous ways to remember the eight great metastories, this book reveals how to include must-have characters into each story, including the hero, nemesis, and mentor (spoiler: smart leaders should not make the dumb mistake of making themselves the heroes of their own stories).

THE SCIENCE AND ART OF STORYTELLING

In September 2008 *Scientific American* published an article by Jeremy Hsu titled, "The Secrets of Storytelling: Why We Love a Good Yarn." You should read the entire article, but here is a summary.

According to Hsu, storytelling, or *narrative*, is a human universal, and common themes appear in tales throughout history and all over the world. The greatest stories—those retold through generations and translated into other languages—do more than simply present a believable picture. These tales captivate their audiences, whose emotions can be inextricably tied to those of the characters in the stories.

By studying narrative's power to influence beliefs, researchers are discovering how we analyze information and accept new ideas. A 2007 study by marketing researcher Jennifer Edson Escalas of Vanderbilt University found that a test audience responded more positively to advertisements in narrative form, as compared with straightforward ads that encouraged viewers to think logically about arguments for a product. Similarly, Melanie Green of the University of North Carolina coauthored a 2006 study showing

that labeling information as "fact" increased critical analysis, whereas labeling information as "fiction" had the opposite effect.

Studies such as these suggest that people accept ideas more readily when their minds are in story mode as opposed to when they are in an analytical mindset.

"I'm looking for a mentor who can show me how to get rich without boring me with a lot of advice."

[CHAPTER 2]
The Simple Six-Step
HEROIC STORYTELLING
FORMULA

The first person to analyze the myths, legends, tales and stories of the world and present a theory of an overarching storytelling formula that resonates across all human societies was Joseph Campbell, in a now-classic 1949 book, *The Hero with a Thousand Faces.* In the early 1970s, a young filmmaker named George Lucas, who was writing a screenplay about space cowboys fighting against an evil empire, picked up Campbell's books and writings on the hero's journey during the course of his own research on stories and was thunderstruck to realize the film he was writing, at the time titled *The Star Wars,* followed the very same motifs and structure. Years later, the two men finally met and became good friends when PBS filmed a multipart series about Campbell's life and work at a little place called Skywalker Ranch. You can't find a much higher recommendation than that.

❶ Start with a main character. Every story starts with a character who wants something. For your story, this is your client—either a real one, or an ideal one. Make your main characters likable so the reader or listener will root for them. To make them likable, describe some of their good qualities and make them relatable.

❷ Introduce a nemesis character. Stories need conflict to be interesting. The nemesis doesn't have to be human; what person, institution, or condition stands in the character's way?

❸ Bring in a mentor character. Heroes always need help on their journey. They need to work with a wise person. This is where you come in. Be the voice of wisdom and experience in your story.

❹ Know what specific kind of story you are telling. Human brains seem to be programmed to relate to one of eight great metastories. These are: monster, underdog, comedy, tragedy, mystery, quest, rebirth, and escape.

❺ Have the hero succeed. In seven of the eight great metastories, the main character needs to succeed, with one exception: tragedy. The tragic story is told as a cautionary tale. (Great for teaching lessons, but not great for attracting clients.)

❻ Give the listeners the moral of the story. Take a cue from Aesop. Don't count on the listeners to get the message. The storyteller's final job is to come right out and tell them what the story means.

EXAMPLE: PATTY VOGAN'S STORY

This tale is told by my buddy, Patty Vogan, who is a Vistage chair in Southern California. Vistage chairs are a worldwide network of executive coaches who bring together successful CEOs, executives and business owners into private peer advisory groups. Patty uses this story to recruit CEOs to join her group.

The funny thing is, when we think about David, we really think about how he went from almost closing his business to realizing his dream of buying a 55,000-square-foot building. The story starts with his peer advisory group at Vistage. We had been working with David about issues of diversification, but it came up a little too short. There came a time when we needed to pull together a tiger team, so we invited five members of the bigger group to come to my house, and I made a big Italian dinner. We digested and worked through his financials, and the tiger team came up with short-term profit centers that he could increase. They also found some really good ideas for expenses to slash and cut for the short term. David continued to work his issues, and his best-practices increased and increased throughout the time he was in the group. He was able to make profit after profit. It is one of those things that we think about—that all leaders have blind spots. David had a huge one, but he was able to come out on top. Eventually, David was able to buy his dream building, and it really is 55,000 square feet. So when we think about it, Vistage works.

It's not *Star Wars,* but can you see the similarities? Patty's story is short and sweet, but it still follows the formula.

1 **Start with a main character**. The main character is business owner David. We like David because of his undeserved misfortune—almost having to close his business.

2 **Have a nemesis character**. In this case the nemesis is a lack of diversification for his business.

❸ Bring in a mentor character. The five-member tiger team, called together by Patty, and that big Italian dinner she made. (Patty cleverly gives credit to the team in the story—not herself.)

❹ Know what story you are telling. This story could be a monster story, a quest story, or an underdog story. But Patty tells it as a mystery. David had blind spots, and the tiger team and the ongoing work with the peer advisors were what cracked the code.

❺ Have the hero succeed. David got his dream: to purchase a 55,000-square-foot building. In storytelling, we call that a *visible finish line*.

❻ Give the listeners the moral of the story. Patty ties a ribbon on the story. All leaders have blind spots, and peers can help you succeed. "So when you think about it, Vistage works."

"I was very ill and my HMO wouldn't pay for human parts."

[CHAPTER 3]
Three Must-Have
CHARACTERS

E very story needs a hero (think main character), a nemesis, and a mentor. If you are familiar with *The Wonderful Wizard of Oz*, the main character is Dorothy Gale of Kansas, the nemesis is the Wicked Witch of the West, and the mentor is Glinda, the Good Witch. (By the way, if I were to write the plot summary for this book and movie, it would be: "Girl arrives in strange land and kills. Makes three friends and kills again." For me, it is the ultimate chick flick: two women fighting over a pair of shoes.)

If the first three *Star Wars* movies are more your cup of tea, then we are talking about

Luke Skywalker as the main character, Darth Vader as the nemesis, and Jedi Knight Obi-Wan Kenobi and later Jedi Master Yoda as the mentors. (My favorite mentor advice from Yoda is: "Do or do not. There is no try.")

Here is more information on the first three steps of the storytelling formula:

▶ **Start with a Hero**. This is the main character. King Arthur, Sherlock Holmes, and George Bailey in Frank Capra's classic *It's A Wonderful Life* all have something in common. They are each the protagonist who propels the story. The first sentence of your story begins with the name of the main character and a clear picture of what he or she wants.

▶ **Next, Introduce the Nemesis**. What prevents your main character from getting what he or she wants? Stories are boring without conflict, so the main character needs opposition from another character. Professor Moriarty ("The Napoleon of

Crime" in the Sherlock Holmes stories) is a master nemesis. So are old man Potter in *It's a Wonderful Life*, the Nazis who want the Lost Ark, and the Wicked Witch of the West in Oz ("I'll get you, my pretty, and your little dog, too!"). Often, the word "antagonist" is a better term. In business storytelling, common nemeses are often government regulations, the competition, or a bad economy.

▶ **Then Add the Mentor**. This is where you come in. Heroes can't do it on their own. They need outside expertise or training. Sometimes they need a gentle hand to show them the way or get them back on the right road. The hero needs the voice of experience and wisdom. Clarence the Angel in *It's a Wonderful Life*, Merlin in the King Arthur legends, and Gandolf in *Lord of the Rings* are there to fill this critical need.

In my workshops, participants often object to being cast as the mentor instead of the hero. "What we did was heroic—we saved that client," they tell me.

"Ah," I tell them, "if you cast yourself as the hero, what role do you give your client?"

The answer is, "the damsel in distress."

Nobody wants to project themselves into a story as the damsel in distress.

Clients want to see themselves as the hero who was smart enough to recognize and listen to the right mentor to help them overcome the nemesis.

Let me repeat this for emphasis: *If you want to attract more clients, then your clients must be the heroes, or main characters, of all your stories* (save one).

▶ Start your story by introducing the main character—*a character like your clients*.

▶ Make the main character likable.

▶ Make people who hear the story want to root for the main character.

Next, you'll introduce the nemesis or problem. In one of my stories, I label a bad economy as "the wolf at the door." If you can use a person to represent the issue—a technique called "personification"—so much the better.

Finally, you should cast yourself as the mentor or wise wizard character of the story. With your training or advice, your hero/client will overcome the nemesis problem. You are the voice of wisdom and experience.

Your presentations, articles, blogs, books, seminars, and speeches should be peppered with such stories. These stories provide the psychological clues as to why prospects should hire you.

So what is the exception? What is the story in which your client is not the hero?

There is only one story you can tell (and never at the beginning of a client relationship) in which you get to be the hero. This is *your* story, which helps prospects understand why they should engage with you.

A FEW FAMOUS HEROES, VILLAINS, AND MENTORS TO GET YOUR CREATIVE JUICES FLOWING

 HEROES/MAIN CHARACTERS

- Luke Skywalker from the original Star Wars trilogy
- King Arthur

- Indiana Jones from *Indiana Jones and The Raiders of the Lost Ark*
- Scarlett O'Hara from *Gone with the Wind*
- Atticus Finch from *To Kill a Mockingbird*
- John Galt from *Atlas Shrugged*
- Harry Potter from *Harry Potter and the Philosopher's Stone*
- Eliza Doolittle from *My Fair Lady*
- Rocky Balboa from *Rocky*
- Katniss Everdeen from *The Hunger Games*
- James Bond from *every single James Bond novel and film ever*
- Cinderella from *Cinderella*
- Lisbeth Salander from *The Girl with the Dragon Tattoo*
- Sherlock Holmes from the Sherlock Holmes stories by Sir Arthur Conan Doyle
- Roy Hobbs from *The Natural*

VILLAINS/NEMESES

- Darth Vader from the original *Star Wars* trilogy

- Wicked Witch of the West from *The Wonderful Wizard of Oz*

- Hannibal Lecter from *Silence of the Lambs*

- Norman Bates from *Psycho*

- Big Brother from *1984*

- Apollo Creed from *Rocky*

- Evil stepmother from *Cinderella*

- Professor Moriarty from the Sherlock Holmes stories by Sir Arthur Conan Doyle

- Judge Banner from *The Natural*

MENTORS

- Glinda the Good Witch from *The Wonderful Wizard of Oz*

- Jim from *Huckleberry Finn*

- Yoda from *Star Wars*

- Professor Henry Higgins from *My Fair Lady*

- Mickey from *Rocky*

- Fairy Godmother from *Cinderella*

- Dr. John Watson from the Sherlock Holmes stories by Sir Arthur Conan Doyle

- Friar Tuck from *Robin Hood*

- Iris from *The Natural*

- Iago from *Othello* (because not all mentors are good mentors)

©Randy Glasbergen
glasbergen.com

"This story about Jack and the Giant...it's really
about you and your boss, isn't it?"

[CHAPTER 4]
EIGHT GREAT STORIES

Next, it's time to decide what story you are telling. As outlined already, there are eight great metastories that humans tell (and want to hear) over and over again. What type of story are you telling? Almost all works of literature follow these eight basic story structures.

This chapter is based on *The Seven Basic Plots: Why We Tell Stories*, a 2004 book by British journalist Christopher Booker which took more than thirty years to research and write. The work is a Jungian-influenced analysis of stories and their psychological meaning. I compared Booker's eight categories and discovered the same rules apply to the greatest business non-fiction books of all time.

Here are Booker's eight categories:

 Monster. A terrifying, all-powerful, life-threatening monster whom the hero must confront in a fight to the death. An example of this plot is seen in *Beowulf, Jaws, Jack and the Beanstalk*, and *Dracula*. Most business books follow this plot. There is some monster problem in the workplace, and this is how you attack it.

Business book examples:

- *The One Minute Manager* by Ken Blanchard and Spencer Johnson

- *Slay the E-Mail Monster* by Mike Valentine and Lynn Coffman

- *The E-Myth Revisited* by Michael Gerber

- *Whale Hunting* by Tom Searcy and Barbara Weaver Smith

- *The Five Dysfunctions of a Team* by Patrick Lencioni

- *Growing Your Business* by Mark LeBlanc

Underdog. Someone who has seemed to the world to be quite commonplace is shown to have been hiding a second, more exceptional self within. Think *The Ugly Duckling*, *Cinderella*, *David and Goliath*, *Jane Eyre*, *Rudy*, and *Superman*. The business books in this category discuss how people raised themselves up from nothing to success—typical rags-to-riches stories. One of my early favorites was *Up From Slavery* by Booker T. Washington; I even got to meet his great-great-grandson and chat about the book.

Business book examples:

- *Moneyball* by Michael Lewis

- *The Art of the Start* by Guy Kawasaki

- *Up the Organization* by Robert Townsend

- *Grinding it Out* by Ray Kroc

 **Comedy**. Comedy and tragedy aren't about being funny or sad; any story can be funny or sad. Comedy and tragedy are about problem solving.

If the main character tries to solve a problem with a wacky idea, that is a comedy. Think of the movies: *Wedding Crashers, We're the Millers, Tootsie,* and *Some Like it Hot.* Following a general chaos of misunderstanding, the characters tie themselves and each other into a knot that seems almost unbearable; however, to universal relief, everyone and everything gets sorted out, bringing about the happy ending. Shakespeare's comedies also come to mind, such as *Comedy of Errors* and *All's Well that Ends Well*, as do Jane Austen's novels, like *Emma* and S*ense and Sensibility*.

Business book examples:

- *2030: What Really Happens to America* by Albert Brooks

- *A Whack on the Side of the Head* by Roger von Oech

- *Purple Cow* by Seth Godin

- *How I Lost My Virginity* by Sir Richard Branson

- *Swim with the Sharks Without Getting Eaten Alive* by Harvey Mackay

 Tragedy. This story is about solving a problem by going against the laws of nature, society, or God. Through some flaw or lack of self-understanding, a character is increasingly drawn into a fatal course of action, which inexorably leads to disaster. *King Lear, Othello, The Godfather, The Great Gatsby, Madame Bovary, The Picture of Dorian Gray, Breaking Bad, Scarface*, and *Bonnie and Clyde*—all are flagrantly tragic.

Business book examples:

- *Too Big to Fail* by Aaron Sorkin,

- *Barbarians at the Gate* by Brian Burrough and John Helyar

- *Liar's Poker* by Michael Lewis

 Quest. From the moment the hero learns of the priceless goal, he sets out on a hazardous journey to reach it. Examples are seen in *The Odyssey,*

Star Wars, The Count of Monte Cristo, The Sting, The Italian Job, and *Raiders of the Lost Ark*.

Business book examples:

- *The HP Way* by David Packard

- *In Search of Excellence* by Tom Peters

- *Influence* by Robert Cialdini

- *How to Win Friends and Influence People* by Dale Carnegie

- *How to Close a Deal Like Warren Buffett* by Tom Searcy and Henry DeVries

- *The Big Short* by Michael Lewis

- *Never Be the Same* by Mark LeBlanc

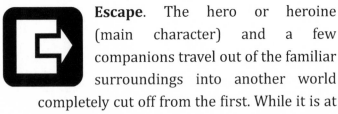 **Escape**. The hero or heroine (main character) and a few companions travel out of the familiar surroundings into another world completely cut off from the first. While it is at first wonderful, there is a sense of increasing peril. After a dramatic escape, they return to the familiar world from where they began.

Alice in Wonderland and *The Time Machine* are obvious examples, but *The Wonderful Wizard of Oz* and *Gone with the Wind* also embody this basic plotline.

Business book examples:

- *The Prodigal Executive* by Bruce Heller

- *The Innovator's Dilemma* by Clayton Christensen

- *How I Raised Myself from Failure to Success in Selling* by Frank Bettger

 Rebirth. There is a mounting sense of threat as a dark force approaches the hero until it emerges completely, holding the hero in its deadly grip. Only after a time, when it seems that the dark force has triumphed, does the reversal take place. The hero is redeemed, usually through the life-giving power of love. Many fairy tales take this shape—also, works like *American Hustle, Beauty and the Beast, A Christmas Carol,* and *It's a Wonderful Life.*

Business book examples:

- *Out of Crisis* by W. Edwards Deming

- *Reengineering the Corporation* by Michael Hammer and James Champy

- *Seabiscuit* by Lauren Hillenbrand (technically a sports memoir)

 **Mystery**. In his book, Booker adds an eighth plot, a newcomer that appeared from the time of Edgar Allan Poe. From the Sherlock Holmes stories to the *CSI* TV series franchise, this basic plot involves solving a riddle, and has gained immense popularity since the mid-1800s. Think of *Atlas Shrugged* by Ayn Rand and the question: "Who is John Galt?"

Business book examples:

- *Good to Great* by Jim Collins

- *Think and Grow Rich* by Napoleon Hill

- *The Secret* by Rhonda Byrne

- *Who Moved My Cheese?* by Spencer Johnson

- *The Monk and the Riddle* by Randy Komisar with Kent Lineback

- *Cracking the Personality Code* by Dana and Ellen Borowka

WHAT'S NEXT?

To improve your understanding and get your creative gears turning, the next eight chapters give you more examples of the eight metastories.

"I'm the monster who lived under your bed when you were
a kid. Got any job openings in your Collections Department?"

[CHAPTER 5]
MONSTER STORIES

There is a horrifying monster that must be killed. This is a kill-or-be-killed situation. Nothing matters more than overcoming the monster. Here is an example from a book my company, Indie Books International, published in 2016, titled *Smooth Selling Forever* by Craig Lowder (some bonus examples from Craig are also included in the appendix). In the book, the clients are the heroes of the stories and Craig is the mentor character.

MONSTER PROBLEM STORY: ROY CHOMKO AND ADAGE TECHNOLOGIES

In 2001, Roy Chomko co-founded Adage Technologies, combining a passion for technology and the desire to build a company focused on driving business value through web technology. As president, Chomko's energy and customer-centric approach have helped to grow Adage into a well-respected, award-winning creator of content-rich websites and e-commerce solutions.

But like any business, there were challenges. Chomko was stretched thin and needed a better sales infrastructure. He knew he needed to change if he was to continue growing fast. Chomko was a rugby player and he knew you won rugby matches by getting the fundamentals right.

As a sales consultant, I helped him install a complete new sales infrastructure. We put sales processes in place, along with performance metrics, a goal and quota-setting system, a structured forecasting process, a hiring system, a format for facilitating productive group and one-to-one sales meetings, and customized his CRM system for activity tracking and performance reporting purposes.

Here is what a smooth selling system and accountability can do in a short time. Adage increased booked orders by 32 percent, forecasted sales by 142 percent, and the sales pipeline by 26 percent during the first nine months of working together. Year-over-year sales increased by 51 percent.

CLASSIC EXAMPLES

Monster problem stories are a staple of literature, plays, and films. Here are a few examples:

▶ ***Jaws*** (novel by Peter Benchley, film by Steven Spielberg). It's a hot summer on Amity Island, a small community whose main business is beach tourism. When new sheriff Martin Brody (main character) discovers the remains of a shark attack victim, his first inclination is to close the beaches to swimmers. That would be bad for the beach tourism and the idea doesn't sit well with Mayor Larry Vaughn and several of the local businessmen (minor nemesis characters). Brody backs down, to his regret, as that weekend a young boy is killed by the great white shark (nemesis). The dead boy's mother puts out a bounty on the shark and Amity is soon swamped with amateur hunters and fishermen hoping to cash in on the reward. A local fisherman with much experience hunting sharks, Quint (mentor), offers to hunt down the creature for a hefty fee. Soon Quint, Brody, and Matt Hooper from the Oceanographic Institute are at sea hunting the great white

shark. A shark is killed, but *that ain't the real monster*. As Brody succinctly surmises after their first encounter with the creature, they're going to need a bigger boat.

▶ ***Beowulf*** (Norse tale from the middle ages). In a medieval land, an outpost is surrounded by an army. A flesh-eating creature called Grendel (nemesis) is killing off all those who live in the outpost. That is, until the arrival of Beowulf (main character), a mysterious mercenary who offers Hrothgar, the outpost's ruler, help to hunt Grendel. Beowulf kills Grendel, but *that ain't the real monster* (notice a theme here?). Beowulf must now fight the real monster, Grendel's evil mother.

"If Robin Hood takes from the rich and gives it to the poor,
then eventually *everyone* will be poor. Explain to me
again why that makes him a hero?"

[CHAPTER 6]
UNDERDOG STORIES

Back in the days of legal dog fighting, the dog that was winning was called the top dog and the dog that was losing was called the underdog. People love to root for the underdog. Here are a few examples:

▶ *Cinderella* (classic fairy tale and two Disney movies). Although the story's title and main character's name change in different languages, in English-language folklore, Cinderella is the archetypal name. The word "Cinderella" (cinders + beauty) has, by analogy, come to mean one whose attributes were unrecognized, or one who unexpectedly achieves recognition or success after a period of obscurity and neglect. The still-popular story of Cinderella continues to influence popular culture internationally, lending plot elements, allusions, and tropes to a wide variety of media. Here is the Disney movie version of the plot (the Grimm brothers' version is more, well, grim): Once upon a time in a faraway kingdom, Cinderella (main character) is living happily with her mother and father until her mother dies. Cinderella's father remarries, and her new stepmother is a cold, cruel woman (nemesis) who has two mean daughters. When the father dies, Cinderella's wicked stepmother turns her into a virtual servant in her own house. Meanwhile, across town in the castle, the land's King determines that his son, the Prince, should find a suitable bride and provide him with a required number of grandchildren. So the King invites every eligible maiden in the kingdom to a fancy dress ball, where his son will be able to choose his bride. Cinderella has no suitable party dress for a ball, but her friends the mice and the birds lend a hand in making her one—a dress the evil stepsisters immediately tear apart on the evening of the ball. At this point, enter the fairy godmother (mentor), the pumpkin carriage, the royal ball, the stroke of midnight, the glass slipper. Cinderella marries Prince Charming, and they live happily ever after.

► ***The Ugly Duckling*** (literary fairy tale by Danish poet and author Hans Christian Andersen, who lived in the 1800s). The story tells of a homely little bird born in a barnyard (main character) who suffers abuse from the others around him until, much to his delight (and to the surprise of others), he matures into a beautiful swan, the most beautiful bird of all. The story is beloved around the world as a tale about personal transformation for the better. When the tale begins, a mother duck's eggs hatch. One of the little birds is perceived by the other birds and animals on the farm as a homely little creature and suffers much verbal and physical abuse from them. He wanders sadly from the barnyard and lives with wild ducks and geese until hunters slaughter the flocks. He finds a home with an old woman, but her cat and hen (nemesis characters) tease him mercilessly and again he sets off on his own. He sees a flock of migrating wild swans; he is delighted and excited, but he cannot join them, for he is too young and cannot fly. Winter arrives. A farmer (mentor) finds and carries the freezing little bird home, but the foundling is frightened by the farmer's noisy children and flees the house. He spends a miserable winter alone in the outdoors, mostly hiding in a cave on the lake that partly freezes over. When spring arrives, a flock of swans descends on the now-thawing lake. The ugly duckling, having fully grown and matured, unable to endure a life of solitude and hardship anymore, decides to throw himself at the flock of swans, deciding that it is better to be killed by such beautiful birds than to live a life of ugliness and misery. He is shocked when the swans welcome and accept him, only to realize by looking at his reflection in the water that he has grown into one of them. The flock takes to the air and the ugly duckling spreads his large, beautiful wings and takes flight with the rest of his new family.

▶ **David versus Goliath.** The account of the battle between David and Goliath is told in 1 Samuel, chapter 17. The phrase "David and Goliath" has taken on the meaning of an underdog situation, a contest where a smaller, weaker opponent faces a much bigger, stronger adversary. In the Bible account, King Saul and the Israelites are facing the Philistines near the Valley of Elah. Twice a day for forty days, Goliath, the champion of the Philistines, comes out between the lines and challenges the Israelites to send out a champion of their own to decide the outcome in single combat, but Saul and all the Israelites are afraid. David, bringing food for his elder brothers, hears that Goliath had defied the armies of God and of the reward from Saul to the one that defeats him, and accepts the challenge. Saul reluctantly agrees and offers his armor, which David declines, taking only his staff, sling, and five stones from a brook. David and Goliath confront each other, Goliath with his armor and javelin, David with his staff and sling. "The Philistine cursed David by his gods," but David replies: "This day Jehovah will deliver you

into my hand, and I will strike you down; and I will give the dead bodies of the host of the Philistines this day to the birds of the air and to the wild beasts of the earth; that all the earth may know that there is a God in Israel, and that all this assembly may know that God saves not with sword and spear; for the battle is God's, and he will give you into our hand." David hurls a stone from his sling with all his might and hits Goliath in the center of his forehead, Goliath falls on his face to the ground, and David cuts off his head. The Philistines flee and are pursued by the Israelites. David puts the armor of Goliath in his own tent and takes the head to Jerusalem, and King Saul sends for David to honor him.

"As my assistant, your job will be to follow me around
humming the 'Jaws' theme every time I enter a room."

[CHAPTER 7]
COMEDY STORIES

I f you try to solve the problem with a wacky idea, that is a comedy. A true comedy usually ends in romance or marriage.

▶ *Tootsie* (film by Sydney Pollack). Michael Dorsey (main character) is renowned in the entertainment field for being a good but difficult and temperamental actor. He is informed by his agent, George Fields (mentor), that no one will hire him because of his bad reputation. In his personal life, Michael is a bit of a cad who treats women poorly, especially his long-term friend and fellow actor Sandy Lester, a doormat of a woman who already has self-esteem issues. Both to prove George wrong and to raise money to finance a play written by his roommate, Jeff Slater, so that he and Sandy can star in it, Michael goes incognito as female Dorothy Michaels and auditions for a role in the soap opera *Southwest General* (wacky idea). The role is Emily Kimberley, the tough, no-nonsense administrator of the hospital. As Dorothy, Michael injects into his audition his own sensibilities, which lands him the short-term role. As Michael progresses in the role, only George and Jeff know Dorothy's true identity. As Dorothy, Michael continues to play the role as he himself would, often ad-libbing. He detests his director, Ron Carlisle (nemesis) for the way he treats "her" and women in general (much the way Michael treated women himself), including Ron's girlfriend, lead *Southwest General* actress, Julie Nichols. Dorothy treats Julie with care and respect and begins to fall in love with her. However, two men fall for Dorothy, namely Southwest General's long time Lothario lead actor, John Van Horn, and Julie's father, Les. Michael has to find a way to let

Julie know his feelings as a man without ruining their friendship. Worse problems arise for Michael when Dorothy's no-exit clause contract on *Southwest General* is extended, meaning Michael may have to pretend to be Dorothy for much longer than he was originally intending.

▶ ***Some Like It Hot*** (film by Billy Wilder). It's the winter of 1929 in Chicago. Friends and roommates Jerry and Joe (main characters) are band musicians, a string bassist and tenor saxophonist, respectively. They are also deeply in debt. Smooth-talking womanizer Joe is a glass-half-full type who figures they can earn quick money to pay off their debts by gambling with the little money they earn. More conservative Jerry is a glass-half-empty type of guy. They are in the wrong place at the wrong time when they witness a gangland slaying by bootlegger Spats Colombo (nemesis) and his men. Jerry and Joe manage to make it away from the scene within an inch of their lives.

Needing to lay low and get out of town, away from Spats, they sense an opportunity when they learn of a local jazz band needing a bassist and a saxophonist for a three-week gig at a luxurious tropical seaside resort in Miami, all expenses paid. The problem? This is an all-girl band—but nothing that "Geraldine" and "Josephine" can't overcome by dressing in disguise as women (wacky idea), the former of whom instead chooses Daphne as "her" stage

name. Sweet Sue, the band leader, has two basic rules for the band members while on tour: no liquor and no men. Beyond needing to evade Spats and his henchmen, and also maintain the front of being women (especially in the most private of situations with the other female band members), Jerry and Joe have two additional problems.

First, the more brazen Joe falls for one of the other band members, ukulele player and vocalist Sugar Kane Kowalczyk (although Jerry, too, is attracted to her). Joe does whatever he can to find time to get out of drag to woo Sugar while in Miami, using all the knowledge Josephine gleans directly from Sugar about what floats her boat in potential-husband material. And second, Jerry, as Daphne, catches the eye of wealthy love-struck Osgood Fielding III, who doggedly pursues "her" and won't take no for an answer. The last line of the movie is one of the greatest in the history of cinema. As Shakespeare would say, all's well that ends well, with this comedy of errors.

▶ *A Funny Thing Happened on the Way to the Forum* (Stephen Sondheim Broadway play and film adaptation, inspired by the farces of the ancient Roman playwright Plautus [251–183 BC], specifically Pseudolus, Miles Gloriosus, and Mostellaria). As the song says, "Tragedy tomorrow; comedy tonight." This screen adaptation of the stage musical of the same name finds the Roman slave Pseudolus (main character) scheming his way to freedom by playing matchmaker (wacky idea) for his master's son, Hero, who is smitten with the blonde and beautiful Philia. But things don't go at all according to plan. The hijinks and complications that ensue involve blackmail, funny disguises, and long-lost children. Pseudolus desperately tries to keep his end of the bargain while a Roman army officer (nemesis) could be the death of him.

"Any of these people would add greatly to our corporate diversity and prove we're serious about going green."

CHAPTER 8

TRAGEDY STORIES

I f a person tries to solve a problem by going against the laws of society or nature or God, then that is a tragedy. The decision to take a shortcut is the tragic decision. As noted earlier, the tragedy doesn't readily lend itself to business stories, because it's a harsh cautionary tale with no room for hope, lessons learned, or redemption until it's far too late for any of the characters, who tend to end up dead in pools of blood at the end due to their own poor decisions or through no fault of their own.

▶ **Othello** (play by William Shakespeare). A 1500s Venetian general, Othello (main character) allows his marriage to be destroyed when a vengeful lieutenant convinces him that his new wife has been unfaithful. Iago (nemesis/mentor), a Venetian army officer and ensign to the Moorish general, Othello, bitterly resents the appointment of Cassio as Othello's chief lieutenant. Roderigo and Iago maliciously bait Brabantio, an old senator, with the news that his daughter, Desdemona, is betrothed to Othello. Before the Council Chamber, Brabantio accused Othello of abducting his daughter to elope with her. The Moor denies this, and Desdemona affirms loyalty to her new husband. Othello is ordered to defend Cyprus, of which he is Governor, against the Turks. Iago (here is the problem—*Othello lets his nemesis also be his mentor*) assures Roderigo, who is also secretly in love with Desdemona, that she will not love Othello for long. Iago brings Desdemona to Cyprus to celebrate Othello's victory against the Turks and incites Cassio and Montano into a drunken brawl. Montano is seriously hurt and Iago beckons Othello, blaming Cassio, who is dismissed from duties. Iago then advises Cassio to seek Desdemona's assistance in regaining Othello's favor. Iago arranges for Othello to find his wife in earnest conversation with Cassio, and subtly arouses the Moor's jealousy by creating a slanderous piece of evidence, placing Desdemona's handkerchief (a very intimate item) in Cassio's possession. Othello's fatal flaw is believing Iago's lie that his lieutenant, Cassio, has been cuckolding him—a lie that leads to a tragic end. Othello ultimately kills Desdemona in a jealous rage and commits suicide himself. Cassio also gets a decent stab in the leg for his pains, and when Iago's wife realizes he's behind the whole thing, she exposes him and he kills her as well. Other bodies pile up along the way as well. Iago himself survives the carnage and vows never to explain why he decided to set in motion all these horrible acts in the first place.

▶ *King Lear* (play by William Shakespeare). King Lear (main character), old and tired, divides his kingdom among his daughters, giving great importance to their elaborate declarations of love for him. When Cordelia, youngest and most honest, refuses to idly flatter the old man in return for favor, he banishes her and turns for support to his remaining daughters. But older daughters, Goneril and Regan, (nemesis characters) have no actual love for him and instead plot to take all his power from him. In a parallel, Lear's loyal courtier Gloucester favors his illegitimate son, Edmund, after being told lies about his faithful son, Edgar. Madness and tragedy befall both ill-fated, but prideful, fathers. They even hang King Lear's court jester (mentor), a fool who spoke the truth to the king.

▶ *The Godfather* (novel by Mario Puzo and film by Frances Ford Coppola). Maybe I like this story so much because this is about a family business; I grew up in a family business and I run a family business called Indie Books International. In the novel and film *The Godfather*, "Don" Vito Corleone (main character), is the head of the Corleone mafia family in New York. The story opens at the event of his daughter's wedding. Michael, Vito's youngest son and a decorated World War II Marine veteran, is also present at the wedding. Michael seems to be uninterested in being a part of the family business. Vito is a powerful man and is kind to all those who show him

respect, but is ruthless against those who do not. When a powerful and treacherous rival (nemesis) wants to sell drugs and needs the Don's influence for the same, Vito refuses to do it. What follows is a clash between Vito's fading old values and the new ways, which may cause Michael to do the thing he was most reluctant to do— wage a mob war against all the other mafia families, which could tear the Corleone family apart. This is how Michael Corleone becomes the tragic hero (new main character) of *The Godfather* trilogy. He makes the tragic decision to join the family business. And although he says it is business and not personal, trust me, it is personal. Unsurprisingly (it's a tragedy), the body count is high, and in the end, Michael dies a broken man, unremembered and alone.

"Be home before midnight, Cinderella.
Your carriage insurance doesn't
cover pumpkins or mice!"

[CHAPTER 9]
MYSTERY STORIES

Whodunnit? Either the audience is in the dark along with the hero, or the audience knows the answer and wonders how and when the main character will figure it all out. Here are examples:

▶ ***The Hound of the Baskervilles*** (novel by Sir Arthur Conan Doyle, plus many film versions). Sherlock Holmes (main character) is a consulting detective in Victorian London. When Sir Charles Baskerville dies unexpectedly, his nephew and heir, Sir Henry, returns from South Africa. Dr. Mortimer, the local doctor, is concerned about Sir Henry's safety, as he is convinced that Sir Charles was literally frightened to death. He consults detective Sherlock

Holmes and recounts the tale of one Sir Hugo Baskerville who, several generations previously, had been killed by a huge hound and which now is believed by some to be a curse on the family. Holmes agrees to take on the case and it almost immediately becomes apparent that Sir Henry's life is in danger. Holmes doesn't believe in the legend of the Baskervilles or the supposed curse placed upon them and sets

out to find a more practical solution. (Interesting story fact: Sherlock Holmes holds the Guinness world record for having been portrayed more times on film and TV than any other character.) Spoiler alert: Holmes cracks the case.

▶ ***Murder on the Orient Express*** (novel by Agatha Christie, film directed by Sidney Lumet). Unexpectedly returning to England from Istanbul in 1935, famed Belgian detective Hercule Poirot (main character) finds himself traveling on the luxury train the *Orient Express*. One of the passengers, Mr. Ratchett, informs Poirot that he has been receiving anonymous threats and asks Poirot to act as his bodyguard. Poirot declines, but when Ratchett is found stabbed to death the next morning, it is apparent that the threats he had received were real. Poirot soon deduces that Ratchett was, in fact, the infamous Cassetti, believed to have been the man behind the kidnapping and murder of three-year-old Daisy Armstrong some five years previously. As he begins to question the dozen or so passengers on the train, he realizes that several of them have a connection to the Armstrong family and he begins to form a solution to a very complex crime. *And the murderer is...*

"Snow White was poisoned by an apple, Jack found a giant in his beanstalk, and look what happened to Alice when she ate the mushroom! And you wonder why I won't eat fruit and vegetables?!"

[CHAPTER 10]
QUEST STORIES

Quest stories are about a journey to find a great prize, or to use Joseph Campbell's word, a boon. Perhaps the prize is to rescue someone, recover something, save the world, or obtain some treasure. Maybe the real treasure is the knowledge you learn along the way. Many memoirs are quest stories. Here are some classic story examples:

▶ ***Indiana Jones and The Raiders of the Lost Ark*** (a film by George Lucas and Stephen Spielberg). The year is 1936. Archeology professor Indiana Jones (main character) narrowly escapes death in a South American temple after obtaining a gold idol—death by poison dart, fall, and finally a giant boulder that chases him out the front of a cave. An old enemy, René Belloq, steals the idol and then orders a group of natives to chase "Indy" down and kill him. Indy, however, escapes back to the United States, where Army Intelligence officers are waiting for him at his university. They tell him about a flurry of Nazi archaeological activity near Cairo, which Indy determines may be related to the possible resting place of the Ark of the Covenant—the chest that carried the original Ten Commandments. The Ark is believed to carry an incredibly powerful source of energy that must not fall into Nazi hands.

Indiana is immediately sent overseas, stopping in Nepal to pick up a relic his old professor had that may hold the key to the Ark's location (and also his former girlfriend Marion, his old professor's daughter), then meeting up in Cairo with his friend Sallah. But danger lurks everywhere in the form of Nazi thugs and poisonous snakes in the Ark's resting place. After Belloq, hired by the Nazis, beats Indy to the treasure again, this time the Ark, Indy and Marion are determined to get it back, and they overpower the pilot of a German plane. But Indy finds himself confronted with a giant German thug, and after a frightening hand-to-hand fight, Indy and Marion blow up the plane. Now the Nazis must drive the Ark to Cairo, but Indy regains control of the Ark after running the convoy off the road, one vehicle at a time. Once again, the Nazis recapture the Ark—and Marion—and head for a Nazi-controlled island. There, Belloq will open the Ark to demonstrate the horrific power it can unleash upon the world!

▶ ***The Grapes of Wrath*** (novel by John Steinbeck, film by John Ford, Darryl F. Zanuck and Nunnally Johnson). After serving four years in prison for killing a man, hotheaded Tom Joad (main character) heads back to the family farm in Oklahoma. Tom is reunited with his family at his uncle's farm only to discover the family must leave that farm the very next day. The extended family packs their belongings onto an old truck and drives to California to look for work. They arrive at an itinerant camp populated with hungry children. A man and sheriff come to the camp promising work but won't say how much they will be paid. The family leaves the camp and arrives at a farm that needs workers. Tom is wary. The farm is surrounding by a barbed-wire fence with plenty of armed guards. The family settles into a shack and picks peaches for five cents a box, earning barely enough to feed the family. Tom kills a thug attacking farm union organizers and has to go on the lam. The family loads up the truck again, hiding Tom under a mattress. They head north and find a camp that is run by the United States Department of Agriculture. Life is better. The sheriff arrives at the camp looking for Tom. Tom vows to his mother that he will fight injustice wherever he finds it, and heads off into the night. The family moves on, hopeful of a better life down the road.

"This book is defective. I tap the
page and nothing happens!"

[CHAPTER 11]
REBIRTH STORIES

What was dead has come back to life. Like a phoenix rising from the ashes, a person or institution is born again. In the Bible it is the tent maker, Saul of Tarsus, on the road to Damascus, becoming the apostle Paul. These stories are about redemption (think Stephen King's *The Shawshank Redemption*). Here are some other examples:

▶ ***A Christmas Carol*** (story by Charles Dickens). On Christmas Eve, crotchety miser Ebenezer Scrooge (main character) is visited by the ghost of his dead partner Jacob Marley. Scrooge is told that what they do in life will determine what happens to them in the afterlife. Marley tells Scrooge that he will be visited by three ghosts (mentor characters) and to take heed of what happens. The first spirit, the Ghost of Christmas Past, shows Scrooge that he was once a happy young man, carefree and in love, but money became his greatest desire. The Ghost of Christmas Present shows him how others, including his nephew Fred and his clerk Bob Cratchit, are spending a poor but loving holiday together, as well as Tiny Tim's crutch by a fireplace. The Ghost of Christmas Yet to Come shows Scrooge the fate that awaits him. Scrooge learns from his visits and becomes a good man who knows how to celebrate Christmas— as well as how to live better all the rest of the year.

▶ *The Parable of the Prodigal Son* (from the Christian Greek Scriptures of the Bible, Luke chapter 15). In my talks, I always say we all come from different faiths. But this story of a lost son is ancient wisdom that can benefit everyone. The story was told by arguably the greatest teacher (and storyteller) who ever lived, Jesus of Nazareth. In the story, a father has two sons. The younger son asks for his inheritance before the father dies, and the father agrees. The younger son, after wasting his fortune (the word "prodigal" means "wastefully extravagant"), goes hungry during a famine, and becomes so destitute he longs to eat the same food given to hogs, which are unclean animals in Jewish culture. He then returns home with the intention of repenting and begging his father to be made one of his hired servants, expecting his relationship with his father is likely severed. Regardless, the father finds him on the road and immediately welcomes him back as his son and holds a feast to celebrate his return, which includes killing a fattened calf usually reserved for special occasions. The older son refuses to participate, stating that in all the time he has worked for the father, he never disobeyed him; yet, he did not even receive a goat to celebrate with his friends. The father reminds the older son that the son has always been with him and everything the father has belongs to the older son (his inheritance). But, they should still celebrate the return of the younger son because he was lost and is now found. (That is where the story ends. We do not know if the older brother, who was righteous in his indignation, forgave his brother and joined the celebration. How do you think the story should end?)

▶ *The Natural* (a movie by Barry Levinson based on a novel by Bernard Malmaud). This is my favorite movie, so that is why it is in the book. Whenever I am sick in bed, I watch this film. Here is the long plot synopsis. The movie opens with a young farm boy, Roy Hobbs (main character), who has an incredible talent for playing baseball (I grew up on a farm with an incredible love, if not talent, for baseball). Encouraged by his father, Hobbs is told by him that he has an amazing gift for throwing a baseball, but he needs more than that if he is to succeed and play in the big leagues. Hobbs witnesses his father's death; he dies while working under a large tree in the front of his home. Some years later, a lightning bolt strikes the tree, splitting it into pieces. Hobbs takes a part of the tree and carves out a bat, using a tool to burn into the bat the name *Wonderboy*, along with a symbol of a lightning bolt for whence it came.

A few years later, Hobbs finds out he is going to get a chance to play in the big leagues. In the middle of the night, he runs to meet his longtime girlfriend, Iris Gaines (mentor), to inform her that he is going to try out for the Chicago Cubs. When he arrives in Chicago, a woman asks Hobbs to confirm what he told her on the train; that he would eventually be the best in the game. When Hobbs agrees, she raises a gun and shoots him.

Fifteen years later, Pop Fisher, the manager of the New York Knights, discovers he has a new "rookie" for his team, a thirty-four-year-old man named Roy Hobbs, whom the team's owner, the stingy Judge Banner (nemesis), has signed for a paltry $500. The Knights begin to rise in the standings due to Hobbs's amazing performance. The lightning bolt on his bat inspires team-mates. Soon after, the entire team adopts the lightning bolt patch, which is worn on their right sleeves. The team's stellar hitting continues, as does the win streak for the Knights. While getting a shoeshine one afternoon, a coach tells Hobbs about the deal that the Judge made with Pop in an effort to swindle the remaining shares from him. If Pop wins the pennant, the Judge would give away his shares. If Pop loses, then the Judge gets all of Pop's shares and he's out for good.

After the game, Hobbs receives a note from Iris requesting to meet with him. Hobbs meets Iris at a café, where they have a cordial visit. Upon leaving, Hobbs asks Iris to come to the next game, but she says she can't for other reasons. After another great game performance, Hobbs leaves the ballpark only to find Iris waiting for him outside. The two walk to her home from the ballpark. During the walk, Hobbs elaborates to Iris about his troubled past and why he failed to return for Iris after leaving for Chicago. At her home, Hobbs notices a baseball glove lying on the couch. Iris informs him it belongs to her son. Hobbs is

shocked to hear this and asks where the father is. Iris says that his father lives in New York (Roy is a little slow on the up-take here).

Hobbs regains his focus, as do the rest of the Knights, and the team begins a winning streak that results in the Knights being three games ahead of the Pirates in the standings for the pennant with just three games to go. The Knights hold a banquet for the team. Confederates of the Judge poison the unsuspecting Hobbs with a tainted piece of food. This results in Hobbs being taken to a local hospital where he is laid up sick for three days. During his visit, the doctor informs Hobbs that his stomach lining has been gradually deteriorating. Upon pumping his stomach, the doctors remove an old bullet that has apparently been there for many years. He is warned if he ever plays baseball again it may be fatal.

Meanwhile, the Knights lose their next three games, allowing the Pirates to catch up and tie with them for first place. Judge Banner visits Hobbs and offers him $20,000 to throw the next game, which will decide who wins the pennant. The Judge leaves Hobbs with the money, assuming that they have a deal.

Iris comes to visit Hobbs at the hospital. Hobbs admits to his failure of falling for the woman on the train all those years ago, and how all of that resulted in his life not turning out how he expected. Hobbs returns to the ballpark the next day, gives the Judge back his envelope of money, informing them all that it's his plan to play in the game that evening.

Hobbs hits a walk-off homer to win the game and pennant. As the team jumps on Hobbs as he crosses home plate, the camera pans to the ball that is still flying out into the night. As the ball drops in the next sequence, it lands in the glove of Iris's son, who throws the ball back to his father, Roy Hobbs, as Iris looks on.

"I laughed, I cried, it became a part of me. I must hire the author to be our next IT consultant."

[CHAPTER 12]
ESCAPE STORIES

Many films have escape right in the title: *Escape from New York, The Great Escape*, and *Escape from Witch Mountain* come to mind. An escape story starts in a normal place, goes to a crazy place, and then the characters must cheat death and make it back to a normal place: home. As Glinda the Good Witch teaches Dorothy Gale in Oz, there's no place like home (could have used that advice when the house landed on the *first* witch, but oh, well). Here are some examples:

▶ ***The Time Machine*** (story by H.G. Welles and adapted into several films). Alexander Hartdegen (main character) is a scientist and an inventor who is determined to prove that time travel is possible. When the girl he loves is tragically killed, Alexander is determined to go back in time and change the past. Testing his theories, the time machine is hurtled 800,000 years into the future. He discovers a terrifying new world. Instead of mankind being the hunter, they are now the hunted, with him stuck in the middle. He must escape the future and get back to his own time.

▶ ***Gone with the Wind*** (novel by Margaret Mitchell and film produced by David O. Selznick). This epic tale of the Old South from the start of the Civil War through to the period of reconstruction focuses on the beautiful Scarlett O'Hara (main character). This story is about escaping the ravages of war. Before the start of the war, life at the O'Hara plantation, Tara, could only be described as genteel (except, of course, if you were a slave). As for the young Scarlett, she is without doubt the most beautiful girl in the area. She is very much looking forward to a barbecue at the nearby Wilkes plantation, as she will get to see the man she loves, Ashley Wilkes. She is more than a little dismayed when she hears that he is to marry his cousin, Melanie Hamilton, and in a fit of anger, she decides to marry Melanie's brother. The Civil War (nemesis) is soon declared and as always seems to be the case, men march off to battle thinking that it will only last a few weeks. Now living in Atlanta, Scarlett sees the ravages that war brings. She also becomes re-acquainted with Rhett Butler (later the mentor character), whom she had first met

at the Wilkes barbecue. Now a widow, she still pines for the married Ashley and dreams of his return. With the war lost, however, she returns to Tara and faces the hardship of keeping her family together and Tara from being sold at auction to collect the taxes. She has become hardened and bitter and will do anything, including marrying her sister's beau, to ensure "with God as my witness" she will never again be poor and hungry. After becoming a widow for the second time, she finally marries the dashing Rhett, but they soon find themselves working at cross-purposes, their relationship seemingly doomed from the outset. Rhett leaves with a classic "Oh, snap" exit line. Scarlett realizes that even if she doesn't get Rhett back, she can always return to the land—to escape back to Tara. As Scarlett says: "Tara! Home. I'll go home, and I'll think of some way to get him back! After all, tomorrow is another day!"

EDITORIAL DEPT.

"We'd like you to condense your novel into something that younger people will want to read...in 140 characters or less."

[CHAPTER 13]
YOUR STORY

Consultants, business leaders, speakers, and authors need to share stories in which they are not the hero. The client or customer needs to be the hero (main character) of the story. There needs to be a villain problem (nemesis) that is holding the client back. Finally, you or your team need to be the wise mentor of the story that helps the client/customer hero overcome the villain problem.

As my buddy Michael Hauge, a screenwriting teacher and consultant to Hollywood film-makers like Will Smith, says: "The story must be true, but it does not have to be factual." In other words, some literary license is allowed to condense the story down to its essence.

WHEN AM I THE HERO?

There is only one story you get to tell where you are the hero. This is your back story, the story that explains why you are doing the work that you do. As an example, here is my back story.

Once upon a time (2001, to be precise), my business coach, Gary Hawk, asked me four questions that changed my life.

First, he wanted to know what the exit strategy was for my San Diego advertising and public relations agency.

"Well, Gary, after I run my firm for ten more years, I am turning it over to someone, and then I will teach consultants and coaches how to attract clients," I said. "My wife and I are going to retire to a college town and spend our life surrounded by trees and water."

His second question was, "How would you do that?" I excitedly told him I would write books, make speeches, put on conferences, and teach at a university. There are so many consultants and coaches that are great at what they do, but no one has ever them taught the science of attracting clients.

Gary said, "You sound very passionate," and then asked his third question. "Why are you waiting ten years to follow your passion?"

That question stumped me, because my thoughts were on my obligations, clients, and employees. I described them as "the wolf at my door." In truth, it was my own fear of failure.

The fourth question helped me process: "How could you get started right now in a small way?"

"I can send invitations for a free monthly lunch seminar in my office," I ventured. "The sandwiches would be on me and I'd share with consultants and coaches the science of finding clients."

My first free lunch-and-learn seminar was the very next month. The invitations were in the mail when the terrorist attack of

September 11, 2001 took place in New York and Washington, DC.

Later that horrible month, much to my surprise, consultants and coaches actually showed up for my lunch seminar. After I explained my theories, the attendees asked how much I'd charge to be their coach. Soon they asked me to write books for them and teach them to give speeches that attract clients. Meanwhile, while five of the top ten advertising and public relations firms in San Diego went out of business, my work helping consultants and coaches to attract clients literally took over my business.

We renamed our company the New Client Marketing Institute. Over the next eight years, I invested $2 million in scientifically researching how to attract high-paying clients. We even tied in with the Harvard Business School. My research revealed a proven way for consultants and coaches to obtain a marketing return-on-investment of 400 percent to 2000 percent. In the next decade, I edited or was the ghostwriter of more than 150 business books (as of this writing, it's now more than 300 business books).

These days, I annually speak to thousands of consultants and coaches, teaching them writing and speaking strategies to attract high-paying clients and how to persuade with

a story. In addition to running the New Client Marketing Institute and the Marketing with a Book and Speech Summits, in 2007, I accepted an academic/administrative appointment as assistant dean and a member of the marketing faculty for continuing education at the University of California, San Diego, my alma mater, a campus located in a grove of trees overlooking the Pacific Ocean.

In 2014, my quest took a new turn. I launched Indie Books International. Independent consultants, coaches, and business owners turn to us for help with the preparation, publication, and promotion of a book that grows their business, puts money in the bank, and helps them make the difference they want to make. Indie Books International was founded by two best-selling authors: Mark LeBlanc and myself. We educate consultants and coaches that the publication of the book is the starting line, not the finish line.

I share my story in order to spread a message of encouragement to consultants and coaches who are good at what they do and need to learn the science of attracting high-paying clients.

The moral of this story is that it isn't really about *me*. It is about *you*. Let me end with four questions for you.

1. What is your marketing with a book and speech strategy?

2. How would you do it?

3. What are you waiting for?

4. How could you get started in a small way?

My suggestion: Start by practicing heroic stories about your clients to include in your face-to-face meetings, speaking, and writing.

Bonus Rebirth Story:
JEFF ROBERTSON AND TEL CONTROL, INC.

By Craig Lowder in *Smooth Selling Forever*

How do you win a battle against bigger, better-known competitors? That was the challenge facing Jeff Robertson, a career public safety official and ex-police officer who was president and CEO of Tel Control, Inc. when he brought me on board as vice president of sales and marketing. Founded in 1969, Tel Control designs and manufactures systems that manage 911 emergency communications at the city, county, and state level.

My task was to participate in a company relaunch, lead the branding effort including the launch of a new product. As a result of the smooth selling system we put in place, the company was able to grow sales by 142 percent within the first six months and secure two multi-million-dollar strategic alliances.

In essence, this was a business restart. The situation was we had to introduce a new product that fit the needs of the market. The company was trying to do this with a direct sales organization competing against entrenched providers. That was a fight we could not win.

So instead of taking the competition head on with a herd of hunters, we tried a different sales tack. Rather than concentrate on direct sales, we changed the focus to selling through channels and building relationships with telephone companies and other 911 emergency communication system value-added resellers (VARs).

The first step in our strategy was to get mind share at these well-established telephone companies and VARs, and that calls for farmers. So we stocked our channel sales team with farmers willing to build and nurture relationships.

We put in a documented sales process, assigned quotas to make sure our revenue-generation plan would be covered, and made sure everyone understood the detailed sales plan. Each quarter we monitored progress to make sure we were on track.

The foundation of this strategy was recognizing that the telephone companies and VARs were already in front of the right prospects. Furthermore, they had the credibility we lacked. The number one job of our channel sales team was to prove to the telephone companies and VARS that going with us would be a safe decision.

Once we convinced the telephone companies and VARs of our 911 system's worth, we became a value-added offering they could propose to their government clients that needed phone systems and upgraded 911 system capability. This did more than just get our foot in the door. These add-on sales helped our channel partners, and it reduced the risk to the governmental public safety organizations because we were vetted by a well-established, bigger brand.

When we acquired two multi-million-dollar strategic alliances, it truly was smooth selling ahead. However, we did not rest. We kept looking to the future.

Craig Lowder is a sales-effectiveness expert with a thirty-year track record of helping owners of small and midsize companies achieve their sales goals. He is the president of MainSpring Sales Group, which assists businesses in need of a strategic sales leader on a part-time contract or project basis to develop and execute a sales strategy, develop sales process and performance management systems, and ensure sales execution. Lowder has worked with over fifty companies and increased first-year annual sales from 22 to 142 percent. He has worked for three Fortune 100 companies: Monsanto, Lucent, and CenturyLink. He speaks extensively on the topics "Smooth Selling Forever" and "Your Sales Should Run Like Clockwork" for Vistage International, the world's largest CEO peer-to-peer association, and other groups and associations.

[APPENDIX B]
Bonus Escape Story:
MARK LEBLANC'S MOM

This is a guest story from my business partner and great friend, Mark LeBlanc.

My dad was sixty-one at the time, still going strong with the two businesses he and my mom owned back in Fertile, Minnesota: LeBlanc Real Estate and Action Advertising. He called me a few weeks before my birthday that year to tell me he had no intention of retiring, that my success had gotten him to thinking that he hadn't quite realized his full potential yet, that he still had at least another ten good years in him, and he was going to give it everything he's got.

On my birthday, my mom called.

"Your dad has had a stroke."

They were taking him to Altru Hospital in Grand Forks, North Dakota.

What's a stroke?

Back then, it was a foreign medical term to me, and there was no time to ask. I cancelled my birthday plans and drove the six hours to Grand Forks. Little did I know that my family's world was about to be rocked to the core.

When we arrived, we went directly to the Intensive Care Unit where everyone had red eyes and could barely talk. It was more serious than earlier imagined, they told us. The danger of losing my best friend was imminent.

I still didn't know what a stroke was.

Within twenty-four hours, I sure did. The doctor called a family meeting and told us in no uncertain terms that Dad was not going to make it, and if by some miracle he did, he would most likely end up in a vegetative state and die in a nursing home.

"You might as well go home now. We'll take care of him from here," the doctor recommended.

Like hell we will. Are you kidding me? This is my dad and best friend you are talking about.

For the next thirty days, we camped out in the waiting room, morning, noon and night. 24/7/30. We took shifts. We answered approximately thirty calls a day to the waiting room. Friends and relatives came and sat with us. More than 500 get-well cards flowed in. After all, this was the one and only Ralph LeBlanc.

He loves to tell that story, and not from the nursing home. Although he was paralyzed on the left side of his body, he was still able to drive, play cards, and even founded a stroke survivors' group in Crookston, Minnesota. But he couldn't work. His dream had died.

Or maybe I should say it was transplanted.

Not long after my dad returned home, Mom called me in tears and about gave me a heart attack. (I knew what that was.) She was crying and asked me if I could please loan her $5,000, and she promised profusely between gulps of air that she would pay me back.

"Don't worry about it," I told her, and overnighted her the check.

Back then (it was only thirteen years ago as I write this), in small towns in northern Minnesota, when couples worked together, the man was usually the lead, and my parents' working relationship was no different. My dad was alive, praise God, but their world would never be the same, to put it mildly. My mom had always been second-in-command, and now she was forced to step up to the plate and assume 100-percent responsibility for their new lot in life.

But this was Lois LeBlanc, up against the wall and soon to be another small-business success story. She was sixty years old and—I would assume—scared to death, although she never let on. She was simply embarrassed to call her son for a loan.

She had two businesses to deal with, and her first decision was easy: dial one down. She cherry-picked a few of the plum clients, but otherwise closed the advertising business.

She focused on the real estate business. And in those ten years that my dad wanted to give it his all, she quadrupled the business. Yes, it's true. Every word of it. Plus, she paid off the mortgage, became debt-free, and put more than $100,000 away for retirement. She bought a new car and paid cash for it. She paid me back the $5,000. I didn't ask for it, but it was hugely important to her to make that payment.

My mom achieved all that success in her sixties, while she was taking care of Dad, who required a fair amount of care. She did it while she also took care of her mother, my grandma

Rudy, who died after a three-year lingering illness.

Did I mention Mom's kidney transplant?

She had one at the age of sixty-four, which meant accomplishing all this in between going to and from dialysis appointments three times a week. Even a kidney transplant didn't slow her down.

Of course, we are all proud of her, and no one more so than Dad. In fact, my dad never misses an opportunity to remind us all that he is the luckiest man in the world, and that Mom is the reason for it.

One day, I finally gathered the nerve to ask her.

"How did you do it, Mom? How did you manage to do all of what you did, under the most extreme and challenging circumstances, at a time of life most people are thinking about retiring?"

She looked at me, as only a mother can look at her son.

"I read your book," she said, and her eyes teared up.

"What?" I was dumbfounded.

"I read your book," she repeated. "I didn't understand half of what you wrote, but I did learn one thing. If someone is not interested in what I have to offer or sell, I realize now that it is not about me. So I don't waste time worrying about it. I move on to the next one."

My eyes teared up, too, at what I now consider to be the highest possible praise for anything I have ever done. And she meant it that way.

Mark LeBlanc, president of Growing Your Business (Mark@GrowingYourBusiness.com), based in Minneapolis, has special expertise on the core issues that business owners and professionals face on a daily basis. His flagship presentation and book, Growing Your Business! *are ideal for addressing how to sell more products and services. People walk away feeling more focused, able to attract more prospects, stimulate more referrals, and ultimately, craft a path and a new plan for generating more business. LeBlanc has been on his own virtually his entire adult life, owned several businesses, and now speaks, writes, and consults on the street-smart strategies for achieving in times of challenge and change. He is uniquely qualified to address audiences of five to fifty to 500 and more, and can deliver an inspirational can-do keynote, a content-rich general session, hands-on workshop, and/or a multi-day program. He is a past president of the National Speakers Association.*

[APPENDIX C]
Bonus Mystery Story:
GARY SCHAFER AND SIVOX TECHNOLOGIES

By Craig Lowder in *Smooth Selling Forever*

When a company is in startup mode, there is the opportunity to start smooth selling from the beginning. That was the case in 2002 for Gary Schafer, a serial entrepreneur with an MBA from Northwestern and a pedigree from McKinsey Consulting. In 2002 he co-founded and became the CEO of SIVOX Technologies, a Chicago area developer of a simulation-based eLearning software solutions targeting Fortune 500 companies with inbound and outbound customer call centers.

When there is no market, a company needs to create one. SIVOX provided software and support services designed to help companies better recruit and train their call-center agents. The company's system, used in about eighty call centers nationwide, enabled call-center agents to practice their call-handling skills through interactive simulations.

As the vice president of sales and marketing, I participated in the launch of this new company. We designed and branded the product as a prepackaged software solution. With the strategy in place, the next task was to hire and train a sales force that could fill the pipeline.

The results were sales of $1.9 million with two Fortune 100 companies (MCI and Sprint) and a $20 million-plus sales pipeline within nine months of launch. We also won the Chicago Software Association's 2003 Early Stage Investment Conference Business Plan Award.

Bonus Quest Story:
JOHN MORGAN AND WINTHROP RESOURCES

By Craig Lowder in *Smooth Selling Forever*

John Morgan, CEO of Winthrop Resources Corporation of Minnesota, is a big Warren Buffett fan.

How big? In 1999 the Berkshire Hathaway Inc. billionaire investor auctioned off his twenty-year-old wallet for $210,000 as part of an effort to raise funds for an Omaha, Nebraska, charity. In the wallet: a stock tip. The winning bidder, Morgan, said he would reveal the stock's name to individuals who gave $1,000 or more to the charity. The Wall Street Journal reported that about 30 people forked over the money,

This is the same Morgan who once bought a portrait of Warren Buffett for $100,000, also for charity. Then in 2011 Morgan bought Buffett's childhood home—where the future Oracle of Omaha lived until age six—and plans to sell it on eBay for $150,100, the Omaha World-Herald reported. There were thirteen bids for the house, which was built in 1923 from a Sears Roebuck kit, and Morgan said he was prepared to pay more if necessary.

I had the pleasure to work with Morgan and bring the smooth selling concepts to Winthrop Resources as national enterprise sales manager. Over a ten-month period, we developed and launched a strategic alliance program that generated $12 million in new sales, along with seventeen new accounts. We also launched a financial marketing program that generated $4.2 million in new sales, along with twelve new business partnerships.

Here's how we did it. Founded in 1982, Winthrop Resources had a singular focus: leasing information technology and capital equipment from all manufacturers, vendors and value added resellers to businesses across a range of industries. When a company buys information technology and capital equipment in the $250,000 to $20 million range, there are two big decisions: what product do we buy and how do we pay for it? We provided several lease financing options that allowed the companies to buy more and leverage the cash-flow advantages of leasing.

When I arrived and assessed the situation it was clear that lease financing was viewed as a highly transactional business, and the focus was on finding technology and capital-equipment buyers that would consider lease financing. Obtaining informal leads from companies like Oracle was not handled in a strategic fashion.

Morgan supported my big idea to develop a formal strategic alliance program with technology and capital equipment sellers like Oracle, SAP, and IBM to help their sales reps close the sale by providing a host of lease-financing options. This took a formalized sales approach to train the reps of the technology companies to close more sales and bigger sales using lease financing as a sales tool. While companies were familiar with the concept of lease financing the hardware, we showed them how software and professional services could be bundled together with the hardware in the lease.

For purchases under $250,000, such as new point-of-sales systems (the modern electronic descendent of the old cash register) for McDonalds, we showed how they could give franchisees more lease options. Partnerships require problem-solving. For instance, we agreed to hold on to the leases, not bundle and sell them to a third party, so if there was a problem they would deal with us.

Bonus Monster Story:
BOB OLIVER AND LUCENT PUBLIC SAFETY

By Craig Lowder in *Smooth Selling Forever*

Bob Oliver, president at Lucent Public Safety Systems in Lisle, Illinois, came to appreciate the importance of organizing people. Oliver was a Northwestern grad who became a career senior-level corporate executive. He was tasked with dressing the company up for sale, but the prospects looked bleak.

Oliver brought me in as vice president of sales and marketing. Immediately it became apparent that the monster challenge at the company was that everybody in sales was trying to sell everything to anybody. As a result, nobody was buying.

The company had multiple product lines that were being sold to entirely different markets. Some products were sold to telephone companies and other products to 911 public-safety answering points (think police departments). Those are entirely different markets that require different selling processes and different types of sales people. As a result, the salespeople, to quote an old saying, were trying to be jacks-of-all-trades and were masters of none. That is the opposite of setting your salespeople up for success.

So we reorganized the company sales department from being a product-centric to a customer-centric one. Which meant sales reps who understood police departments sold market-specific products to those markets and salespeople who understood telephone companies sold products to those markets.

The reorganization of the sales department allowed us to develop a deeper understanding of customer needs, which generated increased sales and reduced costs. This also increased the "stickiness" around customer relationships. Furthermore, it allowed us to take a customer-centric approach to our product development efforts, as opposed to our former product-push approach.

People made the difference because we were able to get the right sales people aligned with the right customers. Instead of one sales team we decided we needed three.

In smooth selling nautical terms, different type boats are needed for different type races. And different types of boats require different crews. (In horse racing parlance, the phrase is "different horses for different courses.")

What were the results? We launched an $8 million call center business. In the two years the company was up for sale we achieved 108 percent and 113 percent of sales plan and I personally secured a professional services contract with a Fortune 100 company valued at $21.3 million over three years.

Bonus Underdog Story: MY MOM

This story is a tribute to my mom, Janice DeVries

She always thought she was lucky to have her birthday on a national holiday. Janice Viola Huff—born during the rock bottom of the Great Depression on February 22, 1931, in Rochester, New York—shared her birthday with the father of the country, George Washington. For decades she enjoyed the day off with family and friends, until an act of Congress created the mash-up Monday holiday in February known as President's Day. I don't think she ever forgave Congress.

On New Year's Eve of 2008, Janice was diagnosed with stage four cancer throughout her body and was given six months at most to live. She lived five more years. Her cancer doctor, Dr. James Long, or Saint Long as she would call him, would eventually call her a medical miracle, and credited her longevity to her positive attitude. She shattered the record for survival on a drug that halts the growth of cancer cells.

She loved her husband Jack, her children, her grandchildren and great-grandchildren, horse races, casino gambling, playing card games, reading modern romance magazines, big earrings, Al Jolson, old-timey country music, and waitressing—probably in that order. Her favorite food was clams, although she was also partial to Lobster Thermidor from a certain Southern California restaurant popular with the racetrack crowd.

Janice judged her life a great success, but overcame great odds to get there. The daughter of Frances Elwell and Allen Huff, Janice was the youngest of twelve children (and also younger than some of her nieces and nephews, and was mortified at school when they respectfully referred to her as Aunt Janice). Her parents separated when she was young, so she was forced by her single mother to become a waitress at the age of thirteen to help support the family during World War II.

Like many in her generation, the war was the defining event of her life. She had five brothers who fought in World War II, including brother Deke who was wounded at Iwo Jima, and brother Ralph who was featured on the cover of *Life* magazine playing taps for the fallen on the D-Day beaches of Normandy. Amazingly, all five survived the war. Along with her mother, Janice was busy with the USO efforts in Rochester. Late into her life she would continue to visit cemeteries on Veterans Day to leave flowers on the untended graves of soldiers she never knew.

She was a wild one. As a young waitress, she was adopted as a mascot by the local Mafia Don who tipped big for side projects ("He had me deliver packages for him," she said).

When she was sixteen the Don asked her what she liked to drink and she quipped: "Beer and Crème de Menthe." A case of each was delivered to her front porch, much to the ire of her mother, who was president of the Rochester Christian Temperance Union. That same year Janice ran away with a female friend to work in New York City, but was arrested by the FBI, jailed ("People were nice; they snuck in cigarettes," she recalled), and was driven back to Rochester by one of her brothers.

The arrest may have been the best thing that ever happened to her, because when Janice turned eighteen, her mother sent this black sheep to live with her father, who was racing horses in Southern California. Shortly after her arrival in 1949, she met a shy twenty-year-old immigrant from the Netherlands, Jack DeVries, who was taking care of horses for his Uncle George and Aunt Carla DeVries. Seeing she was afraid of feeding horses, he helped Janice with her chores. He later said, "I fell for her like a ton of bricks."

The courtship was whirlwind, and on April 2, 1949 they drove to Yuma, Arizona to get married. After a hot dog dinner, they had to drive back to take care of the horses. Nothing would get her down, and racetrack friends (who were legion, from racetrack execs and famous jockeys to tack store owners and grooms) nicknamed her "Tough Huff."

Her greatest assets were a love of people and a gift for gab. A favorite saying was, "People have more fun than anybody." Janice quickly became pregnant, and one new friend named John at the race track in Del Mar, California asked where she was going to deliver the baby. Janice said she didn't know, and he said "You can have the baby at my hospital." He was John Scripps, an heir to the Scripps-Howard newspaper fortune. Janice Frances Ruth "Joy" DeVries (later Swank) was born in January, 1950 at Scripps Memorial Hospital in La Jolla. Jacqueline May "Jackie" DeVries was born September, 1953 in Bixby Knolls, California (near Long Beach), and Henry Jordan DeVries (that's me) was born April,

1957 in Bellflower, California (near Los Angeles).

During the early 1950s, Jack's father and mother returned from the Netherlands and started a dairy farm in Paramount, California. Then Jack and Janice quit the horse racing circuit and Jack worked to help run the dairy.

Janice believed in the value of hard work. To help support the family in the 1950s, she worked as a waitress at a few high-end restaurants, including the Steak House at Knott's Berry Farm. She recalled Walter and Cordelia Knott as tough taskmasters who would only let employees off to vote if they promised to vote Republican. She promised, then went off and voted the Democratic ticket.

She worked hard and played hard. During the 1950s, a photo of Janice and Jack, taken in a luxury box at Hollywood Park with Jack's Aunt Carla, appeared in the society page of the *Los Angeles Herald-Examiner* newspaper. That got Janice into hot water with her employer, because she had called in sick that day; but because they liked her so much, they didn't fire her for playing hooky to go to the races.

In 1960, the DeVries clan moved to Chino, California, where they bought fifteen acres for a dairy farm, horse stables and training track called Chino Downs. During the early 1960s, Jack worked the dairy and also got to follow his passion for horse racing. He trained and raced harness horses at tracks throughout California and Arizona. Watching Jack as a racehorse driver was nerve-wracking for Janice because she had seen her share of horseracing injuries.

Living out in the country was boring for a city gal like Janice. Chino is famous for two things: prisons and dairy farms. We had a dairy farm with a view of the men's prison. (I have to say men's prison, because Chino also has a women's prison and a youth correctional authority; the town is full-service and can incarcerate your entire family.)

In the 1970s, Janice went back to work as a waitress, this time serving lunches at a local country club owned by tennis great Jack Kramer. An avid horse player, Kramer had a special affection for "Janny" because they would bet the horses together. Janice had the sassy, brassy New-York-waitress schtick down. She wore a name tag that said "Sam" ("I don't want customers to know my real name") and developed a loyal lunchtime clientele. When she retired from the country club after twenty-five years of service, they threw a banquet in her honor—a rare tribute for a part-time employee.

During the 1970s, the family sold the dairy farm and Jack became a dairy cattle hoof trimmer (he called it a bovine pedicurist). The greatest part of growing up was my father bringing me into the family business at the age of six; I got to spend every day working by his side on the dairy and later on the hoof-trimming truck. Whenever I pass a compost heap, I get homesick.

Jack and Janice sold their land and moved to Ontario, California. When Jack retired from hoof-trimming in 2000, they sold their home and moved to Vacaville, California to be close to their daughter Joy Swank (who once won a look-alike contest with Janice) and their Swank grandchildren.

After the move to Vacaville, Janice landed a lunchtime waitressing job at the Hungry Hunter in Fairfield, California. A honcho of the chain came to meet her because corporate HQ was appalled a woman of her age had been hired, but he was quickly won over as a fan. She retired from that job in 2003 to take care of Jack, who was recovering from a third bout of cancer.

When Jack passed away in May, 2012, she lost her best friend and soulmate of sixty-two years (and I, too, lost my best friend). But she kept fighting and living in her own home until the final week of her life in November of 2013.

Her motto, taken from a snappy Depression-era song, was: "It's a great life, if you don't weaken." She never did.

Remember that underdog movie, *Rocky,* when the bum fighter's goal was just to go the distance, the full fifteen rounds with Apollo Creed, the heavyweight champion of the world? The character of Apollo Creed was based on Muhammed Ali, thought by many to be the greatest boxer of all time. But not my mom. To my mom, the greatest fighter that ever lived was Joe Louis, "The Brown Bomber," who pummeled Max Schmeling, the uber-fighter from Nazi Germany, in a one-round knockout in 1938.

The night before Mom passed away, she was grumpy with a hospice worker. When the worker left, she spoke sharply to me and said I was supposed to protect her from people like that.

"Mom, she has to do her job," I said kindly. "But, you do look like you went ten rounds with Joe Louis," I added with a grin.

She deadpanned: "I went fifteen rounds."

Yes, you did, Mom. Your final five-year road was rocky, but you, too, went the distance.

[APPENDIX G]
ACKNOWLEDGEMENTS

One day I hope to meet Christopher Booker, author of *The Seven Plots;* next time I am in London, I will attempt to thank him in person. Much gratitude to my business partner at Indie Books International and my fourth-favorite American author, Mark LeBlanc, who wrote the best business quest book I have ever read, *Never Be the Same*. Thanks for the inspiration to all those who anonymously volunteer to write the fair-use plot summaries on the IMDB website. Thank you to my screenwriting and story guru, Michael Hauge, who taught me that it is "Better to write than to get it right," and "The story must be true, but it does not have to be factual." Thanks to my buddy and mega best-selling business author, Ken Blanchard, for inspiring, encouraging, and teaching me (between the two of us, we have sold more than 20 million books).

Thank you to my wife, Vikki Lynn (nee Mondo) DeVries (who trades John Steinbeck quotes with me every day, even if it is just a "woof" from *Travels with Charlie*) and the entire Indie Books International family, especially my daughters, managing editor Karla (nee DeVries) Rosenstein and vice president of client services, Devin DeVries, and the greatest editor I know, Denise Montgomery, our vice president of creative services. Thanks to my sons Jack and Jordan DeVries for stuffing all those envelopes.

Gratitude goes out to my sister Joy Swank for always encouraging me, and to my sister Jackie DeVries for introducing me to Grandpa Roper, her grandpa-in-law, who critiqued my newspaper articles when I was a teenager and gave me the dream of working as a sportswriter for the Associated Press (which I did when I was twenty-one). Thanks to Lou Sauritch, who taught me there is more than one way to get into a press box, and helped me to form my first company at the age of eighteen. Thanks to my childhood sports hero Wally Moon, a 1950s-1960s-era baseball player with a master's degree at a time when most ball players did not even attend college, who has always treated me with kindness and class.

Thanks to the first editor to give me a break: Al McCombs, publisher/editor of the *Chino Champion*, a man with a journalism degree and an MBA, who hired me as a professional writer when I was fifteen, and for four years paid me by the inch published (the same deal Ernest Hemingway once got, but I am not supposed to mention his name and mine in the same sentence).

[APPENDIX H]
ABOUT THE AUTHOR

Henry DeVries is the CEO of Indie Books International, a company he cofounded in 2014. He works with consultants and coaches who want to attract more high-paying clients by marketing with a book and speech.

As a speaker, he trains professionals and business owners on how to sell more services and persuade with a story.

He is also the president of the New Client Marketing Institute, a training company he founded in 1999. He is the former president of an Ad Age 500 advertising and PR agency and has served as a marketing faculty member and assistant dean of continuing education for the University of California, San Diego.

In the last ten years, he has helped ghostwrite, edit and coauthor more than 300 business books, including his McGraw-Hill bestseller, *How to Close a Deal Like Warren Buffett*—now in five languages, including Chinese. He has a monthly column with Forbes.com. He earned his bachelor's degree from UC San Diego, his MBA from San Diego State University, and has completed certificate programs at the Harvard Business School.

As a result of his work, consultants and business owners get the four Bs: more books, more blogs, more buzz, and a path and plan to more business.

On a personal note, he is a baseball nut (his wife calls him an idiot baseball savant). A former Associated Press sportswriter, he has visited forty major league ball parks and has three to go before he "touches 'em all."

His hobby is writing comedy screenplays that he hopes will one day be made into films.

You want name-dropping, he can name-drop. He has worked on projects with Robin Williams; Her Majesty Queen Elizabeth; His Holiness the 14th Dalai Lama; Nobel Peace Prize winners Muhammad Yunus and Al Gore; MVPs and Hall-of-Famers from the NFL, MLB, and NBA; and his three business heroes: Ken Blanchard, Patricia Fripp, and Mark LeBlanc.

To contact Henry to purchase multiple copies of this book or to book Henry as a speaker (or invite him to a baseball game), you may e-mail him at henry@indiebooksintl.com, or call him at 619-540-3031.

OTHER BOOKS BY HENRY DEVRIES

Self-Marketing Secrets (with Diane Gage)

Pain-Killer Marketing (with Chris Stiehl)

Client Seduction (with Denise Montgomery)

Closing America's Job Gap (with Mary Walshok and Tappan Monroe)

Marketing the Marketers

How to Close a Deal Like Warren Buffett (with Tom Searcy)

Marketing With a Book

Made in the USA
San Bernardino, CA
23 March 2017